HANDBOOKS OF EUROPEAN NATIONAL DANCES

EDITED BY
VIOLET ALFORD

DANCES OF BELGIUM

Plate 1   Pas de Maclote. Stavelot, Walloon Country

DANCES of BELGIUM

ROGER PINON AND HENRI JAMAR

NOVERRE PRESS

TRANSLATED FROM
THE FRENCH BY
VIOLET ALFORD
ILLUSTRATED BY
LUCILE ARMSTRONG
ASSISTANT EDITOR
YVONNE MOYSE

First published in 1953
This edition published in 2021 by
The Noverre Press
Southwold House
Isington Road
Binsted
Hampshire
GU34 4PH
ISBN 978-1-914311-15-4
© 2021 The Noverre Press

CONTENTS

Illustrations in Colour, pages 2, 12, 29, 39
Map of Belgium, page 6

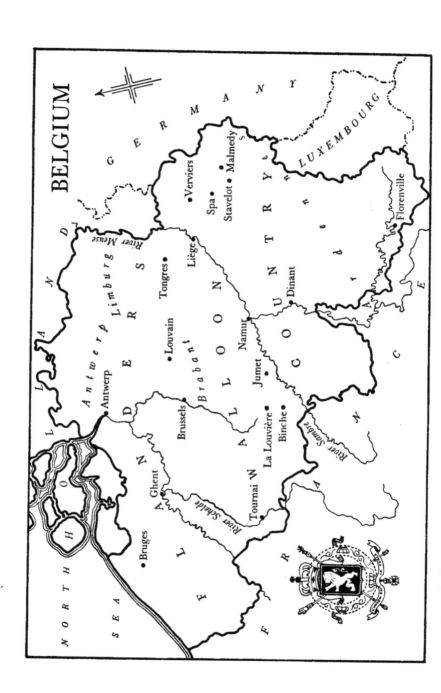

DANCES OF THE
WALLOON COUNTRY
BY ROGER PINON

꧁꧂

The Walloon country is the southern and eastern part
of Belgium in which French dialects known as Walloon are
spoken. This region has its place in the folklore of France,
but in spite of the variety of its different districts one
cannot say it surpasses any of the French provinces in
originality.

The chief occasion for dancing is that of the village fête
on the day of the Patron Saint. Then everybody dances on
the *place*, on platforms called *pontons* or in cafés. 'Balls'
are also held at Christmas, the New Year, at Carnival, at
Midsummer and on St. Martin's Day. Winter, of course,
is the season for indoor dancing.

Certain balls have their specialities; they must take
place out of doors, all the dancers must wear sabots, or
the organisers must scatter scent in the dance hall and
on the dancers, or an official, *un cachet*, must be paid a fee
after a certain number of dances. In Carnival come the
fancy dress balls, everybody masked and disguised. In the
Namur country the local Lord, or the village priest as
his delegate, had the privilege of dancing first. It is a
general tradition that the young men (called *bragards*)
organise the festivities and their Captain has his rights and
duties. He must open the ball, settle quarrels, lead the
Chain dance and fix the sum to be paid by strangers who
attend. In some places he must present a beribboned cock
to the mayor, and round the bird a dance is performed
after its decapitation—a strange and apparently ritual
ceremony known also in the Pyrenees and Spain. The
Dance of la Dorée—the Dorée being a special tart—takes

7

place on the Monday of the fête; the young men, duly preceded by the band, fetch the girls from their homes, an air is played, a dance is danced, the tart, given by the mistress of the house, is eaten and off they go in a Chain with the daughters and the ball begins. 'Picking up' dancers in this way is done nearly everywhere to form the Longue Danse (the famous Cramignon), the Rondes, the Brans, the Galop Chinois, the Trèhes and En Avant deux.*

Our people dance in their own style and with their own manners. When valsing they love to reverse (*distwèrtchî*); the man places his hand, in which a handkerchief is bunched, on his partner's back, thus politely avoiding any soiling of her best dress; on inviting and on leaving her he *fait serviteur*, which means he makes a bow. The lively character of our people shows itself in their love of springing, the men affecting *entrechats*.

SEASONAL AND RELIGIOUS DANCES

In 743 we already find the Council of Leptines prohibiting a dance 'paganus cursus quem yrias vocant'; in 1287 we note the usual medieval dancing in church and churchyard till the dancers fell exhausted—probably part of the dancing epidemics which swept Europe in the thirteenth and fourteenth centuries. From the thirteenth century till 1794 the curious custom known as the Crosses of Verviers, Creûs d'Vèrvî, took people of that town to Liège on Whit Wednesday, there to dance till they were weary in the Cathedral of St. Lambert. Up to the eighteenth century there was still dancing at funerals round Tournai, and in church by the boys of Huy College at the beginning of Lent. Today pilgrims from Jumet to St. Mary Magdalene dance as the escorted procession crosses the *tère al danse* at Thiméon.

* See *Dances of the Netherlands* in this series for the amusing change of this name into Anna van Duinen. *En Avant deux* was once a figure of the Quadrille.

Seasonal feasts have always produced dancing—round the Lenten, Midsummer and St. Martin bonfires; the most interesting are perhaps the Rondes at Malmedy and the Lantern dance (*falots*) at Liège, which we hear of from at least 1478. But all seasonal dances must not be considered ancient. The oldest of the twenty-six airs for the Gilles at Binche for instance is no earlier than 1761. Nevertheless certain elements, such as the bells on their belts and legs and the step itself, seem to be far older. These famous Fools make indeed a highly stylised Spring rite and a wonderful sight they are with their towering ostrich plumes, their clanging bells and their distribution of 'the Luck' in the shape of oranges to the crowd. Nor must we dwell too much on this fruit for it has taken the place of dry bread and onions.

We used to dance and sing round maypoles, and in Gaume little girls still go about each Sunday in May, dancing and singing charming Trimouzètes. These little song-dances show a religious foundation not to be seen in our other dances.

⚜ SWORD DANCES ⚜

Belgium boasts one of the earliest references to the Europe-wide hilt-and-point Sword dance, that of Bruges, 1389. The Sword dance, though it has no connection with the medieval Dance of Death, became known as la Danse Macabrée, confused into Macchabées. It is seen to per-fection in the well-known picture by the younger Brueghel (1564–1638), his Grande Feste de Nostre Village. The dancers are executing the figure Single Under, while, paying no attention to this performance, other people are prancing through a longways Country dance, accompanied by two bagpipers.

The Macabrée is first mentioned at Namur in 1551 and still appears in a degenerate and stylised form at Marbais-en-Brabant and at Waremme, where from 1659 till at least 1880, we find the Donse è Cèke (hoop). This hoop was thrown from the balcony of the Hôtel de Ville— possibly a sunwheel ritual. After this the dance was performed by archers, whose Ronde passed and repassed under the beflowered hoop until all its flowers had been brushed off.

At Dinant in 1562 a distinction is made between the Macabrée and the Jeu d'Espées, while today the former has degenerated into a so-called Pilgrims' dance,* sticks replacing swords.

✻ CHAIN DANCES AND ROUNDS ✻

In the Middle Ages we danced the wide-spread Carole, also the Treske, a word of Germanic origin surviving as Trèhes. The Brans de Fièsse were better known of old than today and we hear of a Chain winding through Liège in 1404. In Hesbaye these Brans are Corôdes, Corantès or Longues danses; at Verviers they are Hièdes à Cawe (tail dances) and all are the Lowlands equivalent of the Provençal Farandole which itself is said to have sprung from the Greek Choros.† Men and women alternate; the leader carries a bouquet or, as in the Cramignon, a stick, souvenir of the Germanic *Leitstab*, that magical, guiding wand. The Cramignon is accompanied by singing, not by instrumental music, and some of our finest traditional songs are those thus used. This dance form is one of the oldest but we get no references to it until the sixteenth century, at Liège and later on at Spa.

The Alion, or Arion, too was accompanied by singing, and was performed in Lent only; its chain circled a figure

* The same thing has happened in Galicia, Spain, where 'pilgrims' use staves for a Sword dance.—*The Editor.*

† See *Dances of Greece* for the Choros and *Dances of France (II)* for the Farandole, both in this series.

made of dough set up on a table—now often replaced by a little girl. The dance was in both chain and longways form, men and women vis-à-vis advancing and retiring to the singing of a *mènwâre* (meneuse or leader), who improvised couplets to a traditional tune.

The Chain dance, Mari Doudouye, burlesque and at the same time magical, took the place, after the introduction of the potato in the early eighteenth century, of a dance to promote the growth of the artichoke. These vegetables were called *canadas* and the potato of today has annexed both dance and name.

The best Rondes are those which necessitate kissing. They are sung or instrumental and very popular are the Rondes of the handkerchief, the neck scarf, the towel and the cushion, all of which are enlivened by a kiss between partners. A sung Ronde, Le Petit Jardin d'Amour, was a favourite during the nineteenth century, but already mentioned in 'La Comédie des Chansons', 1640. Miming Rounds are popular, the best known La Ronde de l'Avoine, our variant of the ancient mime of the growing oats found all over western Europe.

The most valuable to folklore is the Ronde called the Seven Jumps which still ends the fêtes of at least fifty villages in the Entre-Sambre-et-Meuse region. This once magical dance is known from Spain to the Mark Brandenburg of Germany, where the seven jumps took place ritually round an ancient tree.

OLD BALLROOM DANCES

Walloon folkdance embraces and preserves old ballroom dances—at least their names, though the dances which go under the titles may have changed out of recognition— such as the Minuet, the Passe-pied, the Allemande, the Rigaudon and the later Quadrilles and Lancers. Let us also mention La Matelotte or Maclote which is the special

*Plate 2   One of the Gilles de Binche and
Country Costumes, Walloon Country*

dance of the Ardennes, but our whole region once knew it. It probably came from Provence via Paris during the eighteenth century and arrived in two styles. One is the lively, springing style as at Namur, Liège and Stavelot, the other a slower and more graceful style. The first has degenerated into Arèdjes (rages), each variant bearing the name of a village.

OCCASIONS WHEN DANCING MAY BE SEEN

Mardi-Gras (*Shrove Tuesday*)	Dances of the Gilles at Binche.
Mid-Lent	Dances of the Gilles at La Louvière.
Last Sunday in April	Dance of the Society of Archers and their King's Shooting, Marbais-en-Brabant.
Every Sunday in May	Trimouzètes, May songs by girls at Izel and Florenville.
Midsummer Eve and Day	Trèhes and Rondes at Malmedy.
The Sunday after July 22nd	The sacred processional dance of St. Mary Magdalene at Thiméon.
The Sunday after August 15th	La Maclote and dances of the Ardennes at Stavelot. Fête de la Journée Ardennaise.
St. Martin's Eve (*November 11th*)	Rondes round the bonfires at Malmedy and neighbourhood.

DANCES OF FLANDERS

BY HENRI JAMAR

ᴛᴋᴀᴀᴩᴩᴀᴩᴋ

The Flemish part of Belgium comprises all the north of the country, the provinces of Antwerp and Limburg, East and West Flanders and on the south the upper part of Brabant. Both towns and country have a stirring history. The towns have always greatly influenced their neighbouring villages, but those more distant remained for a long time without communications of any sort. Here traditions and manners lived on untouched and their traditional dances existed in good shape up to the end of last century. But after the industrialisation of certain districts too many dances irrevocably disappeared from the knowledge of the people. The powerful Societies of Archers, which existed everywhere, have however preserved their own dances so we must not be surprised to find folk dances on the confines of Brussels and other large towns as well as in the country.

HISTORICAL DANCES

The Moressendans* and the Sword dances were much admired performances especially well known in Flanders. In the ancient town of Bruges the first—in its Court form— was shown in 1468 at the 'rare and solemn marriage of Duke Charles of Burgundy with Margaret, sister of Edward IV, King of England', while the Sword dance was executed in the same picturesque city in 1389 (see p. 9).

Indeed we find records in more than fifty places in the

* We can see Flemish Morris dancers engraved on copper by Israel van Mechlin, *c.* 1470.

14

Campine* as well as in the provinces of Antwerp and Limburg of the *ghesellen van den swerde*. At Tongres, that ancient Roman city, are preserved seven swords belonging to the Sword dancers of St. Michael who last appeared in 1802—without their swords, which had been confiscated during the French invasion. Sword dances generally took place on the first Monday after the Epiphany (the English Plough Monday), on February 2nd, the Feast of the Purification, during Carnival and on other popular festivals.

THE TRAWEITELDANS

This highly interesting dance is performed by one Confraternity† only, in the Antwerp *Campine*. It was evidently once a Sword dance but is now performed with sticks and a hoop, its figures appearing to be a symbolic conference of the brethren during some period of oppression— probably under the Spanish domination. Under the direction of the Captain-Traweitelaar the hoop is passed (on a stick) from one man to another, each entering the hoop by his feet or his head and, bound by this circle, performing the usual Single-Unders or Single-Overs of a hilt-and-point Sword dance. The men turn, press together, jump and close their lines. We seem to be looking at an inextricable knot. This is symbolic of oppression. Suddenly the figure unwinds itself, the hoop slips from one swaying, bending body to another until all are freed from strangling bonds. This is deliverance, the liberation of the Confraternity. A drum roll alone accompanies this strange dance.

* La Campine, Kempen in Flemish, is a once sandy, now lightly wooded, country, agricultural and very conservative.

†The Confraternities are descendants of powerful bodies organised for defence, the most famous being the Archers' and Cross-Bowmen's Corporations. Many of these still live. Others are now occupied in organising village fêtes, sometimes giving the proceeds to the Church. They are usually for men but sometimes for married couples.

We meet the famous Zevensprong, Seven Springs (see p.11) everywhere in Flanders as in the Walloon country and Holland,* performed at every feast. Besides this the Harvest Dance was a favourite before industry invaded the countryside. As in England, when the last load was carried the harvesters decorated the last sheaf, here with red ribbons and flowers and ceremoniously offered it to the farmer's wife. She replied by preparing a feast for all who had helped with the harvesting. The night before she made cakes of the first flour of the year and after a copious meal the harvesters danced the Harvest Dance. This was a couple dance using the ordinary polka step, but there was always one man too many who danced with the sheaf. The couples had barely moved round the room or barn when thud, thud, the directing stick sounded on the floor. Each man dropped his partner and rushed to another. The man with the sheaf dropped it and seized a girl. The new man who was left without a partner had to pick up the sheaf and so the dance continued. Finally the musician so increased the pace that all were obliged to stop, gasping and laughing.

This dance is now done at other times when a broom or a poker replaces the decorated sheaf, and the less invocative names of Polka-stok, Keuterdans or Bezemdans replace the lovely title of Harvest Dance.

SOCIAL DANCES

We also possess a large number of popular dances; indeed in the Limburg and Antwerp countryside there is hardly a village without its own folk dances. As in the Walloon country, we have retained out-of-fashion ballroom dances,

* See *Dances of the Netherlands* in this series for the Dutch version of this dance.

Quadrilles, Lancers, Polkas, Mazurkas, all very cere-
monious. But we have amusing little dances too, the
Klepper-Keuter dances, Hanskens, Molentjes, Hutsepots,
Streeps and so on. They differ from region to region, from
village to village, yet the observer will remark a certain
conformity to each other and to those of other countries.
We must not forget the celebrated Chain dance, sometimes
used ceremoniously, which is found in a few villages along
the Meuse.

MUSIC

In Flanders the Confraternities have faithfully practised
their folk dances for centuries past. It was they who spread
knowledge of them, they who, after a period of decadence,
have succeeded in reviving them. The history of these
institutions shows how, for hundreds of years, dance airs
were used to sustain the spirits of their members. When the
step was grave and firm the drum, with quick beat,
accompanied the dance-song. The triangle too, with its
gay tinkle then came into the corporation *salles*. Later
violins, and at the beginning of this century accordions,
made their appearance. This last is now strengthened with
both wind and string instruments. Directly the ensemble
was strong enough to be well heard the dance-song disappeared and the old words will soon be things of the past.

In the Walloon country the old dancing master and
village musician, the *musiqueûs* or *mèstré*, preferred the
violin and dedicated themselves to their work by crossing
themselves before beginning to play. As everywhere the
accordion has now pushed in. If no instrumentalist was
at hand somebody would provide 'mouth music', singing
a continual tra-la-la to the dance tune. This was called
tarlater.

Our dance-songs, especially those for the Cramignon and
the Rondes, or improvised by the *mènwâre* of the Alion

17

(see p. 10), are not very different from French folk songs and few are truly Walloon. The dancers often repeat the first verse after the leader and also sing the refrain, which arrangement has been compared with the medieval *rotruenges*.

One cannot say that our Belgian composers have often been inspired by their own folk music.

⚜ COSTUME ⚜

There is not a great deal of difference in the costumes from various parts of the country except in details. The men wear dark trousers and the long, blue linen blouse, pleated in the Walloon villages, very full in Flanders, with a red, spotted neckerchief and the characteristic high cap. These are of black or dark blue cloth or silk and never seem to sit comfortably on the head. In the Walloon country the women's skirts are of striped homespun, very sober in greys, blacks or browns and over them are aprons of thicker homespun with horizontal stripes, or plain and short. Their bodices are of cloth or silk with long sleeves. Elbow sleeves are not traditional. Colour is supplied by a Paisley-patterned shawl falling in a short point down the back and at Stavelot by poke bonnets of yellow straw trimmed with gay, check ribbon and a white frill hanging from the back. This is called a *chapeau à bavolet*. The skirts here may be in gayer colouring. In Flanders the women's caps are noteworthy. They are of beautiful lace, sometimes with ear-flaps, sometimes with two long ties floating down the back. (White caps can also be seen in the Walloon villages.) Skirts are of the same striped material and often have a frill to make the hem stand out, or many lines of seams across the cloth for the same purpose.

Sabots are worn for working and used to be danced in. Nowadays only the dance groups wear their old costumes, especially the Confraternities who dress with pride and care.

Before the last war the Confraternities were the only bodies which practised traditional dances and that only at their full sessions. After the war several dance groups were organised, all having the same aim—to preserve and to reinstate our folk dances. Most of these groups belong to the 'Volksdanscentrale voor Vlaanderen', and are chiefly for young people.

OCCASIONS WHEN DANCING MAY BE SEEN

St. Anthony's Day (January 17th) St. Sebastian's Day (January 19th) St. Barbara's Day (December 4th)	All these are fête days of the Confraternities named after these saints; dancing also takes place on other days of patron saints of the Corporations.
Mardi-Gras (Shrove Tuesday)	Masking and disguises and dancing.
Anniversaries of the foundation of Confraternities	Several Corporations meet in a village and pay the 'price' of dances with a good deal of disputing.
At Flemish Kermesses (fairs) and other popular fêtes	The Chain dance is danced at the end of the Kermesse. The date differs from village to village.

⚘ *NOTE* ⚘

The first fourteen books of this series contained a plea to respect the costumes represented, to copy them with care and exactitude when needed to perform the dances, and not to introduce fantasies. It is disappointing to read reviews of these books in various papers now recommending our illustrations for 'fancy dress'. This is precisely what they are not. Regional costume is a heritage and the pride of the people to whom it belongs.

The Editor

THE DANCES

TECHNICAL EDITORS

MURIEL WEBSTER AND KATHLEEN P. TUCK

ⵜⵓⵎⵎⵜ

ABBREVIATIONS
USED IN DESCRIPTION OF STEPS AND DANCES

r—right ⎫ referring to   R—right ⎫ describing turns or
l—left ⎰ hand, foot, etc.   L—left ⎰ ground pattern
C—clockwise   C-C—counter-clockwise

For descriptions of foot positions and explanations of any ballet terms the following books are suggested for reference:

A Primer of Classical Ballet (Cecchetti method). Cyril Beaumont.

First Steps (R.A.D.). Ruth French and Felix Demery.

The Ballet Lover's Pocket Book. Kay Ambrose.

Reference books for description of figures:

The Royal Scottish Country Dance Society's Publications. Many volumes, from Thornhill, Cairnmuir Road, Edinburgh 12.

The English Folk Dance and Song Society's Publications. Cecil Sharp House, 2 Regent's Park Road, London, N.W.1.

The Country Dance Book I-VI. Cecil J. Sharp. Novello & Co., London.

POISE OF THE BODY AND HOLDS

WALLOON COUNTRY

1. In La Maclote unless stated otherwise the woman holds her apron with both hands while the man lets his arms hang naturally.

2. Old fashioned waltz grasp.

3. Cross grasp.

4. Side grasp. In this partners face each other with the arms lifted sideways to shoulder level to grasp each other's hands.

5. Wheel grasp. The dancers start with the r (or l) hands grasped across to form the spokes of a wheel.

6. Circle grasp. With hands joined round to form a circle.

FLANDERS

Several of the dances in Square formation have a certain solemn pose. Quadrilles, Lancers, the Polka Salué and other dances require bows and bob-curtsies with hands on hips. Couples often walk arm in arm.

1. In turning together in Couple dances the man holds his partner with his hands on her hips; she places her hands on his shoulders.

2. When advancing the man places his l hand on his partner's back and she places her r hand on his back. The free hands are joined in front well forward.

3. When stepping in line all have hands on hips.

BASIC STEPS

WALLOON COUNTRY

Crossed Polka Step (La Maclote)

	MUSIC
1 Spring on to whole of l foot across and in front of r foot.	*Beats* 1

2 Cross r foot up behind l foot. | and

3 Spring on to l foot with r foot raised high and crossed behind l foot. | 2

4 Hold this position. | and

This step is then repeated with the r foot on beats '3 and 4 and', so that there are two full crossed polka steps to a bar.

N.B. The step is well marked when raising the leg behind and the body leans a little forward.

Walking Step (Mari Doudouye)

This is taken with a swagger.

Glissé

This is a gallop or slip step and can be taken travelling sideways in the usual way or travelling forward, in which case one foot is kept in front and the other is drawn up behind with each spring.

FLANDERS

Ordinary walking or polka step may be used.

Spring Waltz (De Kegelaar)

Danced to six-eight time and very like a pas de Basque sauté, i.e. springing. But it is danced with poor technique and the knees are not lifted although they give easily with the movement. It can also be danced turning. In six-eight time there will be one step to a bar, i.e. Spring on to r (or l) foot. | 1-2

Momentarily take weight on to ball of l (or r) foot. | 3

Spring again on to r (or l) foot. | 4-6

Repeat, springing on alternate feet.

LA MACLOTE

Region	Stavelot (Plate 1).
Character	Very gay and quick, raising the knee in some steps.
Formation	Four couples standing vis-à-vis, the lines about four yards apart; each man on L of his partner. (O=woman, □=man.)

Dance	MUSIC Bars
Musician plays A music.	A
FIGURE I	
4 crossed polka steps forward, half-turn to L.	1–2
4 crossed polka steps forward, half-turn to L bringing all dancers back to their own places.	3–4
FIGURE II	B
8 crossed polka steps forward, lines meeting.	5–8
8 crossed polka steps backward.	5–8
FIGURE III	A
Partners face with cross grasp.	
8 pas glissés turning on spot C.	1–2
8 pas glissés turning on spot C-C.	3–4

23

LA MACLOTE

Arranged by Arnold Foster

Play three times as written

FIGURE IV | B
5–8

Each man changes places with his partner with 8 crossed polka steps. They pass l shoulders and make a half-turn to the L to face each other again.

Repeat back to places. | B
5–8

FIGURE V | A
1

All move forward into square with 2 crossed polka steps.

Join r hands in wheel grasp and take 4 pas glissés C. | 2

Join l hands in wheel grasp and take 4 pas glissés C-C. | 3

Return to places from the square moving backward with 2 crossed polka steps. | 4

FIGURE VI | B
twice

Repeat Figure IV.

This Maclote is followed immediately by a second.

SECOND MACLOTE

Formation   As in First Maclote (see diagram).

Dance

Musician plays A music.

FIGURE I | A

As in Figure I of First Maclote.

FIGURE II | B
twice

As in Figure IV of First Maclote.

FIGURE III
A

Couples join in old-fashioned waltz grasp. They turn on the spot C-C with 16 pas glissés making 3 turns.

FIGURE IV
B twice

As in Figure IV of First Maclote.

FIGURE V
A

As in Figure III of First Maclote.

FIGURE VI
B

Couples 1 and 3 move forward into a square with 2 crossed polka steps and take circle grasp. — 5

All move together C with 4 pas glissés. — 6
All move together C-C with 4 pas glissés. — 7
Both couples move backward into own places with 2 crossed polka steps. — 8

Couples 2 and 4 repeat this figure. — **B** 5–8

FIGURE VII
B twice quicker

Partners join with side grasp. With 8 pas glissés couples cross with one another, couples 1 and 3 together and 2 and 4 together. Then with 8 pas glissés return to their own places.

FIGURE VIII
A

Partners change to old-fashioned waltz grasp and turn to L on spot with 8 pas glissés. — 1–2

Each man places both hands on his partner's waist and lifts her (she springing) across him to his R side. — 3–4

SECOND MACLOTE

Play A B B, A B B, A B B. *then* B B A *at quicker tempo* (♩ = 126)

MARI DOUDOU*r*E

❦❦❦❦❦❦❦❦

Region   Court-Saint-Etienne; Walloon-speaking Brabant; round Namur and in the region of
Entre-Sambre-et-Meuse.

Character   Lively and amusing giving an opportunity for
all to meet, sing and process.

Formation   A procession of couples; in some places it has
become a single file chain dance. The leader
sings the verses, dancers and onlookers join in
the refrain. The men dance with bare feet,
the women wear shoes.

Dance

A swaggering walking step, bodies swaying. At the
words 'et non-na!' every dancer must make a complete
turn or pirouette. (Those who fail to turn on the exact
beat are fined. With the fines the dancers pay for a litre
of liqueur which is passed round as a loving cup. If a
woman refuses to drink, a dummy soaked in the liqueur
is forced into her mouth. These dummies are love
charms which girls wear hung round their necks.) The
'promenade' continues ad. lib.

❦❦❦❦❦❦❦❦

Great big turnips
To fill her white baskets
And then we plant out our
   potatoes
With you, Mari Doudouye, with
   you Mari Doudouye—oh no!
We promise you
Mari Doudouye—oh no!

Now in our village
And in your hamlet,
See us all feasting
On our potatoes
As we praise Mari Doudouye.
Then there is dancing,
They're dancing barefoot
In honour of Mari Doudouye
On the red flagstones.

Plate 3   De Kegelaar, Flanders

MARI DOUDOUYE

Arranged by Arnold Foster

DE KEGELAAR (*The Skittle Player*)

Region   The Limburg Campine (see p. 14).

Character   Gay and rather fast. All sing as they dance.

Formation   A circle formed by six (or more) couples standing round at equal distances apart and facing the centre. All have hands on hips. (O=woman, □=man.)

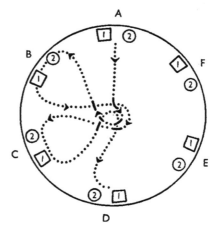

Diagram shows track of A1 to two women, B2 and C2, and on towards D2. This track is repeated with each woman in turn.

Dance	MUSIC
	Bars

FIGURE I

    A1 and A2 dance 4 polka steps forward to the centre of the circle.   **1–4**

    The man holds his partner with his hands on her hips, she has her hands on his shoulders. In this position they turn C on the spot with 4 polka steps.   **5–8**

    A1 now moves towards B2 with 4 walking steps.   **9–10**

    They turn together with l arms linked.   **11–12**

    A1 then continues with 4 walking steps towards his partner who, meanwhile, has moved into the centre of the circle using Spring Waltz steps, and is ready to meet him.   **13–14**

    They turn together with r arms linked.   **15–16**

    A1 has now completed the figure of eight which will be repeated with each woman in turn. They remain in their places allowing A1 to come to them.

FIGURE II

    A1 moves towards C2 with 4 walking steps.   **1–2**

    They turn together with l arms linked.   **3–4**

    A1 moves towards A2 with 4 walking steps.   **5–6**

    They turn together with r arms linked. The woman's movements are the same as in Figure I. The man has now completed a second figure of eight.   **7–8**

FIGURE III

    Repeat as in Figure II with D2.   **9–16**

These figures are repeated by each man in turn.
The dance is started again by the women who
will then dance the figure of eight with each
man in turn. To finish, the music is played
much more quickly for eight bars or so.

DE KEGELAAR

Arranged by Arnold Foster

Allegretto ♩. = 108

HANSKE VAN LEUVEN (*Louvain Johnny*)

Region   Provinces of Antwerp and Limburg (Plate 4).

Character Happy and rather quick. The dancers sing as
          they dance.

Formation Lines of 3 facing each other; one man between
          two women all holding hands. As many lines
          as desired.

Dance   This is a progressive dance. A springing
          walking step is used or a pas de waltz.
          (O=woman, □=man.)

F	O	□	O	F
E	O	□	O	E
D	O	□	O	D
C	O	□	O	C
B	O	□	O	B
A	O	□	O	A
	1	2	3	

	MUSIC *Bars*
Lines A & B, C & D, E & F, balance towards and away from each other.	1–2
A2 and A3 join hands in a circle with B3 and all move round together C; meanwhile B1 and B2 join hands in a circle with A1 and all move round together C-C. (Bars 3 and 4 are used to give hands in the circles.)	3–4 5–8
The two men change places.	9–10

HANSKE VAN LEUVEN

Arranged by Arnold Foster

37

Repeat the circles as in bars 5–8 but with A2 in C-C and B2 in C circles. End in own place in lines.	11–14
Balance in lines as in bars 1 and 2.	15–16
The two men A2 and B2 turn together C with waltz steps while each woman does the same with her vis-à-vis. End in own place in lines.	17–20
Balance in lines as in bars 1 and 2.	21–22
The three dancers in line B make two arches by raising their joined hands. A2 and A3 pass together under the arch made by B2 and B3. Meanwhile A1 passes alone under the arch made by B2 and B1. In this way the lines change places. After waiting one turn line B will join the dance again repeating the movements of line A.	23–24

These movements are danced at the same time by lines C & D, E & F. When line A has reached the bottom of the set the movements are repeated until they are back in their original place at the front of the dance.

LOUVAIN JOHNNY

Johnny, don't you ever get married
Or you will be miserable.
Johnny, don't you ever get married
Or you will rue it.

Plate 4   *Hanske van Leuven, Flanders*

BIBLIOGRAPHY

✦✦✦✦✦✦✦✦✦

THE WALLOON COUNTRY

CLOSSON, ERNEST.—The MS. speaks of *Basses Danses de la Bibliothèque de Bourgogne*. Société des Bibliophiles, Brussels, 1912.
——*Chansons populaires des provinces belges*. Brussels, 1905, 1912, 1947.
DEFFET, J.—*Danses anciennes. Danses du pays de Liège*. Liège, 1895.
DENEUFBOURG, Alp.—*Le carnaval de Binche. 25 airs de Gilles*. Binche, 1930.
GOFFIN, S. and LEJEUNE, E.—*Danses ardennaises*. Liège, *c.* 1945.
LEBIERRE, Olivier.—*La Lyre Mâmediéne*. Leipzig, 1901.
LIBIEZ, Albert.—*L'originalité des chansons d'Alion*. Brussels, 1951.
MONTPELLIER, Ernest.—*La danse à l'épée, dite danse macabrée*. Namur, 1937.
POLAIN, Eugène.—*Les cramignons liègeois*. Liège, 1927.
ROUSSEAU, Félix.—*Légendes et coutumes du pays de Namur*. Brussels, 1920.
TERRY, L. and CHAUMONT, L.—*Recueil d'airs de cramignons et de chansons populaires à Liège*. 1889.

References to folk dance and costume are rare even in publications specialising in folklore. The reader should turn to Reviews such as *Wallonia, Le Bulletin de la Société Royale, Le Vieux-Liège, Le Guetteur Wallon, Le Folklore Brabançon* and so on.

For costume see various articles in *Les Enquêtes du Musée de la Vie Wallonne*, Liège.

FLANDERS

BLYAU, A. and TASSEEL, M.—*Iepersch oud-liedboek* [songs]. Ghent, 1900.
BOLS, Jan.—*Honderd oude vlaamsche Liederen* [songs]. Louvain, 1897.
CORNELISSEN, J. and VERVLIET, J. B.—*Ons Volksleven* [folklore].
JAMAR, H.—*Boerenvreugd en Boerenleed* [folklore]. Oostham, 1943.
LAMBRECHTS LAMBRECHT.—*Het oude volkslied, Limburgse Liederen* [songs]. Ghent, 1937.
LOOTENS, A. and FEYS, J. M. E.—*Chants populaires flamands* [songs]. Bruges, 1879.
SIMONS, Jozef.—*Ons vroom en vroolijk Kempenland* [On the Campine]. Antwerp, 1925.
STERKENS-CIETERS, Dr. Paula.—*Volkskleederdrachten in Vlaanderen* [costume]. Antwerp, 1935.